# HUSH

THE HOUGHTON MIFFLIN
NEW POETRY SERIES

Judith Leet, *Pleasure Seeker's Guide*
David St. John, *Hush*

# David St. John

# HUSH

*Houghton Mifflin Company Boston 1976*

Some of the poems in this book originally
appeared in *Apple, Cincinnati Poetry Review,
Field, Fuse, Kayak, The Nation, The Ohio
Review, Poetry Northwest,* and *Transpacific.*
"For Lerida" and "Slow Dance" were first
published in *Antaeus,* and "Iris," "Hush,"
"Dolls," and "Gin" originally appeared in *The
New Yorker.* Some of the poems also appeared in
the chapbook *For Lerida,* published by the
Penumbra Press (special thanks to Bonnie
O'Connell).

The quotation from Paul Éluard is taken from
*Uninterrupted Poetry: Selected Writings of Paul
Éluard,* translated by Lloyd Alexander (New
York, New Directions, 1975).

*Library of Congress Cataloging in Publication Data*
St. John, David, date
Hush.   I. Title.
PZ4.S1424Hu    [PS3569.A4536]    811'.5'4    76–15998
ISBN 0–395–24673–3
ISBN 0–395–24672–5 pbk.

Printed in the United States of America

W  10 9 8 7 6 5 4 3 2 1

*for Vivian and for David Wyle*

*for Fran*

Are we two or am I all alone     — PAUL ÉLUARD

# Contents

# THIS

AFTER TADEUSZ RÓŻEWICZ

This is the light, I said.
This is the light, and the day.

The boy looked at me, his face
the color of dust. It's not enough,
he said. You're lying. There's more.

This is the street, I said.
This is the street where people walk,
the street they see from their windows.
It is this one.

He saw a waitress
wetting her lips with her tongue.
Yes, he said. Go on.

This is a house. Someone's home.
There's a fire going, dinner on the table.
There are children waiting: for a father,
a brother back from the war. For a silence
in the keening. For the beds to warm
themselves, in winter.

Never, he said. I don't believe you.

Here; I pointed. A newsman
whose tongue is a rancid almond. A machinist
whose ears drone like sirens. Your own twin,
looking for a street sign. A girl, slipping
her hands under your shirt.

No, he said. Go on.

These are my hands,
that drag a knife through meat,
that stack crates in warehouses, in trucks,
that whisper like thieves in dark offices,
that twist an icepick into your temple,
that hold a woman's face.

Yes. What else.

Nothing else. Or this:
that some days, the letter you wait for comes;
that the light is blowing into the hallway —
as you open the door, and step out.

You're lying, he said. Go on.

# NAMING THE UNBORN

Once more,
sweet milk fills
my woman's breasts;

the moons of her nipples
darken, and rise.

Her waist thickens,
and the cloud inside her belly

swirls around our second child.

A small bean of flesh,
he floats toward life;

all the rivers of her body
empty into his eyes,

her blood drums from his mouth,

already we
have named him.


\*


In his third month,
he broke

into stillness,

7

his world gave up
and began to drift away;

his silence bled from the womb.

\*

Afterwards,
his face rose in our dreams
like a planet,

and we said:

you,
broken tear,

little star of red mud,

flesh-blown and milky;
you, Joseph.

## RUINS

In each brick,
a dark egg swelled
and rocked;

the shingles
curled into wings
and flew off,
the two-by-fours
bent their backs into prayers.

Spears of herb grass
drilled the sunlit
veins.

The roof's
crucifix a rust of crumbs.

How do I enter
or return?
Through which airy
doorway
shaking my key
of fingerbone,

to my bed,
filling with leaves.

# THE EMPTY DANCE HALL

Resin swirls across the floor.
The country band has left;
and a mandolin
still sits in a window,
half a wooden pear.

The dry boards creak and pop,
the brass chandelier clinks softly.

I take the mandolin, and go out
under the ivy arbor,
and the swaying canopy of oak.
A folding chair falls shut
on the patio;
on the dark, uneven bricks.

I lean in the doorway,
and slide my fingers along
the rosewood neck.

As I begin to play
the wind rises,

like a girl
getting up from her chair,
for the last dance.

# ENDLESS LETTER TO SOUTH BAY

The squirrels
still rattle in the attic;

the hard pods
of the fir spray their yellow salt

across the lawn.
The stone fireplace,
streaked with dust and soot.

The amber window, dark again.

Another night in your old house,
writing another endless letter.

Dear G,
each new line
dangles from my teeth
like a black string.

My words disappear,
like gravel
tossed in a lake —
sinking
through the pages of water.

# COMING HOME

Walking through the drugged afternoon
through the slender hallways

of my country,

I weave and bend like water grass —
that unsure, suspicious —

I shuffle
the old shuffle
through these cities,

these forests, by rivers
that run like the lines
along my hand:

following the rivers,

following tracks printed in the mud
by any animal,

holding my thumbs before me,

and following them anywhere;
collecting moss and lichen for no reason,

collecting no lovers' names.

In fields of low grass
my friends are singing

*take me up*
*take me in your arms* . . .

\*

I kick up stalks and crescents in the dust.
At a town's edge,

a girl stands on a hotel terrace

unbuttoning her jacket
stitched with milky poppies, and her workpants

smeared with diesel grease and sperm.

As I go by, she turns;
shivering. As night carefully blackens the land.

\*

Some place along the way, I kneel
for a long time under a flayed eucalyptus.

Coming home.

## ALONE

I go out on the porch
and watch a firefly weave
through the pines — lost Saint,
stone lantern, looking
for the way.

The slow wheel in my chest
turning, I sit at the card table,
and trace your hair in the blue
dust of my saucer. The rib of moon
sails on.

The sun drops into
this valley. The leaves on the maple
lift, and shiver in the morning —
like the thin dresses in a closet
you're opening, somewhere.

# ORANGE

Tonight, loneliness or winter
so perfect, I cut open an orange
and read the news of old affections,
friends, beliefs & lies left home as
we fled and set sail for a new world.

Here's a necklace of water, seeds
of awe, childhood: rust-black. Names abandoned
or given back — son, Broken Bow, future, bastard, sir.
Lavish dolls, & fear's message: witch * touch * faith.
Day-raids & sack lunches, desks, fresh orange,
cloud, cloud.

      My father peels hemispheres,
and hands me a world lucent, naked, & orange.

## FOR GEORG TRAKL

Your face,
so pale now it is blue.
And in the icy, dead moons
of your eyes, the things you
loved are trembling; all
utterly blue —

The small, soft breasts
of your sister. Vienna's night — alone;
frosted stairways. Blue sonata, blue rosary
of morning, blue sun. The river, and the sleek
angel stepping from its waters, offering
a robe of woven larkspur.

And the azure pearls
of opium, asleep in your palms —
as if, from the glazed balcony
of your cheeks, blue tears
had fallen.

# DYING

In a field by
my house, I lie in the furrows,
a child in my father's room, pulling
the blankets closer, and closer —

Who could bruise the sleep of boxes?

Nights, my prayers
dust thin faces: the sly martyr in her child's
coat, the vain suicide who grabbed his knapsack
and came with me to the Mid-West.

— Once I matched drinks
with a friend until the floor snapped,
and I went at the walls with a penknife
carving a dream of grotesques.

Whose smile breaks like mercury?

Let me stand in fog
by the Pacific, walk the shore of ferns,
and drift —

　　　Let my son
put his tiny, rough fingers on my eyes.

## FOR LERIDA

Clove, salmon knocking
in the pot; flames waking
off blue wood. A bottle
of Spanish wine squats on
the table. The sad radio
talks of herons rising out
of the Capital, of pianos
blown to dice, of trains
ticking across the borders,
towards this city. I touch
the bruises, shadowed pink
with make-up, around her eyes.
She tells her dream: a street
like milk, painted with new
snow. Of a house where it is
always winter; her sister
fluttering down hallways like
a paper corsage. The spoons
her mother ties to her dresses
spilling always with a pale
dust, or heroin. Her lover
in a blond raincoat, slipping
thin, quiet fingers into her
rings; and leaving. — Outside,
the river is howling its prayers.
A last moon is packing its bags.

# FOUR O'CLOCK IN SUMMER: HOPE

AFTER THE PAINTING BY TANGUY

Something that, in a glance, could be a plump
featureless canary, caught sitting in mid-air.
It's breast, swelling; a stretched wing, or cloud.
Or simply: a humped & yellow amoeba, disguised
as a gentleman's rakish hat, blown off the pier —
tumbling along this parfait seafloor. Perhaps.

It's true; we must decide. *Is* there a horizon?
Is the sky squatting on the earth, or a dark cloud?
Or is the sky diving into the sea, & the sea licking
its own hills? Or, is this a lake that has fallen
onto another lake? Why, & if: these underwater clouds?
At some point, we must decide. Is shore horizon —

This landscape keeps passing through itself.
Everything that moves — bird, land & weather — changes.
The cafés soften. Ash waves along these boulevards.
The city folds to a single bud — A green light pouring
across the windows. The chocolates, & violins, begin
to sweat, & sour. Walls leak. We give it up, & go.

Among these slightly bloated shapes, & shifting
historic dunes. The certainty of the mirage, as it
appears. Out into an atmosphere of dust, & dusk; sure
that it's some image of ourselves we sail out to greet.
The harbor empties. The waves are littered with light.
Those vague curls have fallen across your shoulders.

A shirt flags in the wind. Like a small boy peeing
off the back of a rowboat, we know a life dissolving
in its past, and a future passing back into its life.
We build a bridge of waves over the waves, & drift on.
Already, we can see a rider turning his horse to face
the breakers & a girl who has captured the sunlight

in a cage of quartz walking home to her grey father.
Some are certain now a shore surrounds these waters.
That the lake has begun to calm, & the marshes smooth.
Others are more hesitant; they've seen a single branch
reaching out of a fog, its thousand fingers shaking —
an applause of nerves. The lazy drone; nothing.

\*

We've lost our yellow hat, our suitcase. Perhaps
the hat unfolded its wings, & dove off the side of
the boat. Perhaps it was bored with its shabby stool.
Perhaps our Captain left the sinking ship. We try,
God knows, doing the best by our world. But lately,
there are tales of ties strangling haberdashers.

You've put on your Garbo perfume. Our old books
have never smelled so sweet, the old movies seem so
true. I've plotted our escape to the villa — Italian
sunlight breaking in the window slats, the dance
floor rustling its gown of new parquet. There's only
one thing left to do. Sweep you off your feet.

Those who give up finally give up too much.
You're the one suicide who stays a friend. What you
ask is simply nothing but that's simply never enough.
To wait there, as you pointed the skiff into a storm,
I vowed to take up my affair with your mandolinist.
I took off my silence, & my coat; & I waited for you.

Have you fallen in love with our room? The view
of the fog shuffling over the bay, the bare masts
by the pier spelling an old loneliness. Have you
tied up your hair with the last ribbon? Is that my
notebook you've filled with drawings, & with things
like, "The window darkened as he broke the pane."

What we have left is what we had. Our pale bodies.
There was an inn at the edge of a forest, & we ate.
There were orioles asleep on our terrace, for days.
In the room there was a Chinese mobile, spiting
an absent wind, & touch; counting its glass fingers,
& the days left. Who's left these delicate notes?

Who's taken my yellow fedora? Will the Bentley
pull up beside the curb again, as you toss wild rice
at the pigeons? Does this mean you'll never write?
Are these seasons leaves of our musty books? Haven't
you another day? Will you live on the yacht? Can't
you mail the paintings? Don't you want the dulcimer?

*

Lerida, there's a compass in the desk, a map.
We have days, the stars, & luck. Let's chance it.
Let's tack a blanket to some pole, & fall asleep.
There's a cold that starts in certainty; I'm sure.
And now I'm cold. You see? The farmhouse shivers
in this wind. Papers catch the drafts, & sail.

I've found a spider web. Hold out your hands.
It's a puzzle that begins that night your father
walks the orchards & takes the night by its lapels.
A man leaves his life; neighbors talk. You promised
you wouldn't follow, remember? A pale lace in a branch.
Why does smoke leave ash? — Hold out your hands.

Pull up the quilt, let's count the scraps from Russia.
Here's the Paris print, great-grandmother's splurge.
Ours is a heritage of rags. Uncle's kerchief. Suppose
a wheel on their horsecart snapped. Would we have missed
each other? Our mothers riveting wings to airplanes,
1942. They'll never make it. Not pulling that cart.

It's past noon, & the weather can't hold. We could
go climbing. Shall I hook the sidecar to the Harley?
Make me confess: that I'd forgotten the Greek alphabet.
That I'd torn up my tickets. That your canary flying
out of my pocket was enough. If I were shy, I'd say:
I've fallen for a girl who paints parrots on her parasol.

I've bandaged the suitcase, & packed the leather trunk
with books. There's a train tonight, at 4. White trees
on the stationery of our Hotel. In your tender script,
we'll write an old romance: A girl who tosses Father's
spats out of a biplane, & the boy who finds them. They
meet by chance — she, emptying a basket of black leaves

off a balcony; he, stepping out of a fortune teller's
wagon, in his new spats. Of course, leaves cover him.
He is amazed. She drops her basket on the steps, & we
know the ending has forgiven us — These luxuries are
simply dawns. Lerida, when we arrive, the Hotel's fine
shades will draw. Our deskman tips his lemon derby.

# ELEGY

They've carried the fat man who yelled
For more butter on his lobster through the streets
Weeping. No, not the man the people are weeping & a whole city
Is domed with auroras & smoke. The fat man's dead.
Only the sea is silent about it, everyone else
Is carrying on, & the pucker of lye & revolt washes the rough
Mouth of the harbor. That man walked his mornings
By the shore. He dragged a brazen,
Wooden woman in off the beach, & nailed her
To the thick beam of the ceiling, where she looked out
For bad weather & Chile. Hung the wall with a ship's
Wheel, so that the moon lit the brass & copper spokes
     & such an odd star
Led him back, always, to this room overlooking the waves.
The sign of the crab shifts across the horizon. The sorrow
Of night. He is laid out like an old sea lion,
Not so much exhausted as worn: Of taking
That chance of saying what pleases you, such as the truth.
Or some few words that sound like music & the sea.
That please you. That come & go.
As easily as a government of tides, or the vandals & soldiers
Sacking your house. As the blossoms of lilac draping the casket.
Of all simple things, the simplest: Your lashes
Locked together. A little earth.

# SIX/NINE/FORTY-FOUR

KEITH DOUGLAS (1920–1944)

The black windows. Her arms,
pocked as the streets. The old man
drags a folding chair onto the fire escape,
to watch the sky. He says it's like the night
he gave up the marimbas for a woman
in an apricot gown dancing by the bandstand.
The air begins to swirl with a pink & white
dust of plaster & bricks. The old man
picks up his boater, & broken hand-mirror.
A sailor with no lashes, & a pearl
necklace, mimes
the moment his wife dipped their son's
foot into a bowl of tepid, sudsy water & all
hell blew apart & these quills of porcelain
into his face. Outside London,
a sleepy girl in a cakeshop is undisturbed
again by anything.
On a wedding cake, she repeats the two forks
of a road joining, lazy V's of lime & lemon icing.
She soft-shoes, & unties her apron. A long walk
home, & very late.

\*

In North Africa, they
mark the crossroads with blank stones,
as if the stones were there first.
The chaplain's leading
services & a corporal playing
the hymns on a saxophone. The lizards,
& anise in the wind. At the camp's
edge, a wild dog rummages under canvas,
into the shallow graves. In Cairo,
his whore flips off a taxi driver & pukes,
& refuses tea. She says, Ice cream. A large man
in a white suit admires his own hands, & pours
his sherry into the blue rose on his table.
In Alamein, a censor dumps his scotch
over an orange sliced in a glass, & holds up
a poem typed on an aerogram, & can't decide.
He blacks the line about a Second Front,
& the rhyme of *tits* with *spits*,
& knows now it doesn't scan, but who gives
a fuck. Someone whose friend's
dressed in a greatcoat & a dog's face,
a friend leaning on his shoulder the long way
from Morocco to the Continent. Along the boat's
rail, & coughing. To a ragged
France, the slow clack of blood, & a soft,
black window in his gut. No poem, & drawings
in his pocket. A loosed bête noire. The third day
of Normandy. Keith Douglas.

*

The open window. Her arms,
pocked as the streets. The tea steeps
in the tin pot. Across the way, the theater
marquee flushes. She leans on the sill,
watching a sullen ticket girl press
her face against the faces
of a poster. She lays out the morphine
syrettes, & pours the tea, & puts a picture
of him in Cairo, a café's rag awning
shadowing his eyes, in a wood box by his poems.
As the newsreel begins, speeches & the applause
of guns drift over. The globe
of the radio's dial floats
out of its cabinet, a smoldering planet.
She turns the squat arrow like a deft & staunch
compass — Across the threads of line dividing
the world in a pie of vague hums, the endless
static of hymns, & days. A woman out
walking her dog
in a cemetery begins to laugh very loudly,
& uncontrollably. In the cherry orchards, the dead
branches, & stones the birds have left.

*

My father has fallen
asleep in the Shangri-La. The jukebox
sticks, & at the bar a blond bitches
ships & shipyards, the grease she scours
off her hands with kerosene. The bartender
polishes, & nods. She says her taste for fast
cars & martinis has gone.
A man kicks the jukebox, & my father lifts
his face off the cold table,
& straightens his flight jacket, & his cap.
He walks into the glare of the California
afternoon; & like blood on the page
of your detective novel, or a rude drunk rising
like a bruise — I hold up 2 pictures. Look.
A fourth Xmas, at my father's feet. My face
a moon above the blue dark of a sailor's suit.
The blond curls like a pin-up girl's
across my forehead. Now this: the slick,
leather-shouldered pilots standing by the hard
wheels of a B-17. And these sons
putting their faces to pillows as cold
as a father's leather chest.
These sons picking through the silences
of abandoned Quonset huts, where they were born.
These fathers: suddenly air. Blown from cockpits
into the shrugs of sons, the shrugs of my friends
& poets; all of us walking out of these pages,
& the wars, & these fathers. I've fallen

asleep in the same Shangri-La.
Asleep in my father's old overcoat.
The woman beside me has a sour mouth, a sour
kiss. Poetry
deserves legacies. In France, it's nearly
afternoon, & I'm broke. Dead drunk. Very late,
& a long walk home.

# FOR PETER EVERWINE

The white silk jacket tossed
on the guitar, the silk slacks crumpled

in the finch's cage. Your song has undressed,
& stepped out of the window into the bare arms

of the olive. Around your eyes, tracks of muddy
terns, & gulls. A man walks his fields by the sea.

Evening, the tamarisks. The squirrels
high in the pines, bitching at a red moon. Quilts

in the grass, the damp book of meat, curds of cheese—
A woman cradling the dulcimer like a slim, blond

daughter. Dear Peter, with the seedless hive
of a pomegranate, & the oyster-shell comb I dragged

through my mother's hair; with an oriole's split
beak, & the grace of a weed; the pucker of my son's

mouth, his absence; with the spokes of maple leaves,
& the spines of moths — with these,

I'll make a field
at dusk, where the marsh birds are drifting

down, as an old man forgets his story. The psalms
& mandolins, Peter; the silence.

## SLOW DANCE

It's like the riddle Tolstoy
Put to his son, pacing off the long fields
Deepening in ice. Or the little song
Of Anna's heels, knocking
Through the cold ballroom. It's the relief
A rain enters in a diary, left open under the sky.
The night releases
Its stars, & the birds the new morning. It is an act of grace
& disgust. A gesture of light:
The lamp turned low in the window, the harvest
Fire across the far warp of the land. The somber
Cadence of boots returns. A village
Pocked with soldiers, the dishes rattling in the cupboard
As an old serving woman carries a huge, silver spoon
Into the room & as she polishes she holds it just
So in the light, & the fat
Of her jowls
Goes taut in the reflection. It's what shapes
The sag of those cheeks, & has
Nothing to do with death though it is as simple, & insistent.
Like a coat too tight at the shoulders, or a bedroom
Weary of its single guest. At last, a body
Is spent by sleep: A dream stealing the arms, the legs.
A lover who has left you
Walking constantly away, beyond that stand
Of bare, autumnal trees: Vague, & loose. Yet, it's only
The dirt that consoles the root. You must begin
Again to move, towards the icy sill. A small
Girl behind a hedge of snow
Working a stick puppet so furiously the passers-by bump

Into one another, watching the stiff arms
Fling out to either side, & the nervous goose-step, the dances
Going on, & on
Though the girl is growing cold in her thin coat & silver
Leotard. She lays her cheek to the frozen bank
& lets the puppet sprawl upon her,
Across her face, & a single man is left twirling very
Slowly, until the street
Is empty of everything but snow. The snow
Falling, & the puppet. *That girl.* You close the window,
& for the night's affair slip on the gloves
Sewn of the delicate
Hides of mice. They are like the redemption
Of a drastic weather: Your boat
Put out too soon to sea,
Come back. Like the last testimony, & trace of desire. Or,
How your blouse considers your breasts,
How your lips preface your tongue, & how a man
Assigns a silence to his words. We know lovers who quarrel
At a party stay in the cool trajectory
Of the other's glance,
Spinning through pockets of conversation, sliding in & out
Of the little gaps between us all until they brush or stand at last
Back to back, & the one hooks
An ankle around the other's foot. Even the woman
Undressing to music on a stage & the man going home the longest
Way after a night of drinking remember
The brave lyric of a heel-&-toe. As we remember the young
Acolyte tipping
The flame to the farthest candle & turning
To the congregation, twirling his gold & white satin
Skirts so that everyone can see his woolen socks & rough shoes
Thick as the hunter's boots that disappear & rise
Again in the tall rice

Of the marsh. The dogs, the heavy musk of duck. How the leaves
Introduce us to the tree. How the tree signals
The season, & we begin
Once more to move: Place to place. Hand
To smoother & more lovely hand. A slow dance. To get along.
You toss your corsage onto the waters turning
Under the fountain, & walk back
To the haze of men & women, the lazy amber & pink lanterns
Where you will wait for nothing more than the slight gesture
Of a hand, asking
For this slow dance, & another thick & breathless night.
Yet, you want none of it. Only, to return
To the countryside. The fields & long grasses:
The scent of your son's hair, & his face
Against your side,
As the cattle knock against the walls of the barn
Like the awkward dancers in this room
You must leave, knowing the leaving as the casual
& careful betrayal of what comes
Too easily, but not without its cost, like an old white
Wine out of its bottle, or the pages
Sliding from a worn hymnal. At home, you walk
With your son under your arm, asking of his day, & how
It went, & he begins the story
How he balanced on the sheer hem of a rock, to pick that shock
Of aster nodding in the vase, in the hall. You pull him closer,
& turn your back to any other life. You want
Only the peace of walking in the first light of morning,
As the petals of ice bunch one
Upon another at the lip of the iron pump & soon a whole blossom
Hangs above the trough, a crowd of children teasing it
With sticks until the pale neck snaps, & flakes spray everyone,
& everyone simply dances away.

# IRIS

VIVIAN ST. JOHN (1891–1974)

There is a train inside this iris:

You think I'm crazy, & like to say boyish
& outrageous things. No, there is

A train inside this iris.

It's a child's finger bearded in black banners.
A single window like a child's nail,

A darkened porthole lit by the white, angular face

Of an old woman, or perhaps the boy beside her in the stuffy,
Hot compartment. Her hair is silver, & sweeps

Back off her forehead, onto her cold & bruised shoulders.

The prairies fail along Chicago. Past the five
Lakes. Into the black woods of her New York; & as I bend

Close above the iris, I see the train

Drive deep into the damp heart of its stem, & the gravel
Of the garden path

Cracks under my feet as I walk this long corridor

Of elms, arched
Like the ceiling of a French railway pier where a boy

With pale curls holding

A fresh iris is waving goodbye to a grandmother, gazing
A long time

Into the flower, as if he were looking some great

Distance, or down an empty garden path & he believes a man
Is walking toward him, working

Dull shears in one hand; & now believe me: The train

Is gone. The old woman is dead, & the boy. The iris curls,
On its stalk, in the shade

Of those elms: Where something like the icy & bitter fragrance

In the wake of a woman who's just swept past you on her way
Home

& you remain.

# HUSH

FOR MY SON

The way a tired Chippewa woman
Who's lost a child gathers up black feathers,
Black quills & leaves
That she wraps & swaddles in a little bale, a shag
Cocoon she carries with her & speaks to always
As if it were the child,
Until she knows the soul has grown fat & clever,
That the child can find its own way at last;
Well, I go everywhere
Picking the dust out of the dust, scraping the breezes
Up off the floor, & gather them into a doll
Of you, to touch at the nape of the neck, to slip
Under my shirt like a rag — the way
Another man's wallet rides above his heart. As you
Cry out, as if calling to a father you conjure
In the paling light, the voice rises, instead, in me.
Nothing stops it, the crying. Not the clove of moon,
Not the woman raking my back with her words. Our letters
Close. Sometimes, you ask
About the world; sometimes, I answer back. Nights
Return you to me for a while, as sleep returns sleep
To a landscape ravaged
& familiar. The dark watermark of your absence, a hush.

## DOLLS

They are so like
Us, frozen in a bald passion
Or absent
Gaze, like the cows whose lashes
Sag beneath their frail sacks of ice.
Your eyes are white with fever, a long
Sickness. When you are asleep,
Dreaming of another country, the wheat's
Pale surface sliding
In the wind, you are walking in every breath
Away from me. I gave you a stone doll,
Its face a dry apple, wizened, yet untroubled.
It taught us the arrogance of silence,
How stone and God reward us, how dolls give us
Nothing. Look at your cane,
Look how even the touch that wears it away
Draws up a shine, as the handle
Gives to the hand. As a girl, you boiled
Your dolls, to keep them clean, presentable;
You'd stir them in enormous pots,
As the arms and legs bent to those incredible
Postures you preferred, not that ordinary, human
Pose. How would you like me? —
Leaning back, reading aloud from a delirious
Book. Or sprawled across your bed,
As if I'd been tossed off a high building
Into the street,
A lesson from a young government to its people.
When you are asleep, walking the fields of another
Country, a series of shadows slowly falling

Away, marking a way,
The sky leaning like a curious girl above a new
Sister, your face a doll's deliberate
Ache of white, you walk along that grove of madness,
Where your mother waits. Hungry, very still.
When you are asleep, dreaming of another country,
This is the country.

� ✿ ✿ ✿

# WEDDING PREPARATIONS IN THE COUNTRY

This is a poem like a suitcase
Packed with flour. The baker eloping
With his lover insists on making his own wedding
Cake. Or, the mime in whiteface penciling his brows.
The white marble tombstone that Jude
Left blank, save
For the star more like a man's hand with the fingers
Spread than any star. In other words,
What is bleak is a table covered with snow, & the man
Beside it sipping coffee on his terrace
With a woman who is pale with anger pointing a pistol out
Across the blank, white lawn. Now the boy in whiteface
Delivers his bouquet: Cold lilies perhaps,
But more likely he tosses the limbs of a drama onto the terrace,
Or a few Chinese roses, & the promise of despair
Is as reliable as winter. As a suitcase spilling on the stairs.
The cake! Those squibs of icing,
Those stars squeezed from the nozzle of a paper cone
Onto these broad fields of cake.
The sorry stone admits that something's gone. Or someone.
Someone like you. Like the little man & woman riding
The cake. Close the suitcase. Go back down the snowy stairs.

# GIN

There's a mystery
By the river, in one of the cabins
Shuttered with planks, its lock
Twisted; a bunch of magazines flipped open,
A body. A blanket stuffed with leaves
Or lengths of rope, an empty gin bottle.
Put down your newspaper. Look out
Beyond the bluffs, a coal barge is passing,
Its deck nearly
Level with the water, where it comes back riding
High. You start talking about nothing,
Or that famous party, where you went dressed
As a river. They listen,
The man beside you touching his odd face
In the counter top, the woman stirring tonic
In your glass. Down the bar the talk's divorce,
The docks, the nets
Filling with branches and sour fish. Listen,
I knew a woman who'd poke a hole in an egg, suck
It clean and fill the shell with gin,
Then walk around all day disgusting people
Until she was so drunk
The globe of gin broke in her hand. She'd stay
Alone at night on the boat, come back
Looking for another egg. That appeals to you, rocking
For hours carving at a hollow stone. Or finding
A trail by accident, walking the bluff's
Face. You know, your friends complain. They say
You give up only the vaguest news, and give a bakery
As your phone. Even your stories

Have no point, just lots of detail: The room
Was long and bright, small and close, angering Gaston;
They turned away to embrace him; She wore
The color out of season,
She wore hardly anything at all; Nobody died; Saturday.
These disguises of omission. Like forgetting
To say obtuse when you talk about the sun, leaving
Off the buttons as you're sewing up the coat. So,
People take the little
They know to make a marvelous stew;
Sometimes, it even resembles you. It's not so much
You cover your tracks, as that they bloom
In such false directions. This way friends who awaken
At night, beside you, awaken alone.

## RIVER

It distracts you, history. The more personal,
The more confused. You keep moving as the water moves,
Without a motive, taking every irrespective turn
Against the grain. The hotel leans at the edge
Of the bank, a few spare trees —
You'd say, No, I never waited here for coffee,
For a woman so hopelessly petulant with her gifts.
The mornings, smoking cigarettes. The fishermen sliding
Past the cove. Touch them: these ribbons of moss
Hanging in the trees like a woman's hair.
Remember. Now, watch the river wash the shore. How
The sand is taken, only to be put down later, there . . .
Casual sailboat circling underneath the bridge.
Maybe she thought you must stay silent or lie, alone.
That what you kill in yourself, you kill in others —
Or maybe, just the other way around.

# SCARVES

How you compose me, drunk
Of winter, & we survive. These scarves
You drape across me, casual & limp as dirt —
A complicity, & warmth. A friend's last
Indiscretion: you're always right, or you
Put your supper into my lap. (Your cough
Has stopped, the rough woolens packed away.)
We supposed: I am the last poem of vodka,
& you dance slowly to yourself. "Like a girl
Who'd steal a motorcycle," you undress. How
Winter wrecks a garden. Blisters, & rouge.
(We took a razor to the wallpaper.) How as
I hit you a feather of blood broke along
Your lips. You weave into your scarves wings
Of a stuffed finch, & a postcard of a slipper.
As your daughter crawls between us, soft bug
Of nonchalance. There's a strange burlesque
Out in the trees. Again; & the leaves are not
Cruelty, brushing our cheeks.

# THE COLOR OF SALVATION

You go along in your life,
Until even the furniture speaks its regrets.
The fields whipping
The sunlight across the sky, the birds sucking
Water off the leaves. Every pastoral
Hunger, or cure. Your last friend refuses to walk
In her own time,
Leaving you only the climate of other centuries,
The beautiful prayers, & lies. Each morning, thinking
Of an old poem, she says —
Remember the nighthawk flying  in the window
Of the meadhall, & out again? How that one moment
Was all of life, everything
After or before just a black prism, eternity? Yes,
You remember, & the room takes on the attitude of milk
Boiling in the sun. Or,
Your face turning to meet hers. Its pale wash, flush
Of salvation; its fast & human shade.

## YOU

Lean out of the boat, & pick
A dead bird off a wave. A bird black
With oil. The head rolls gently, in your lap,
As we

Sail for an hour back toward the shore,
Bitter,

Tired of quarreling. The way
I put the boat too close to the rocks, & spit
At the sun. How this annoyed you, made
Your legs turn inward. The day is special
In no way. Yet, it's the day your life changes,
& starts to matter. To no one else,
Or for any delicate reason, but simply
Because you reached far
Out of the boat, to pick a dead bird off a wave.

What you say matters. What I say sounds
Ridiculous. Yet, it has to do
With you. How I stood on the railing
Of the balcony, reaching high into the lime tree
Because you wanted
Your gin with lime. Well, loneliness means having
Your gin neat, & style's the passion
Of carving away your life from other lives,

& risk is just a vehicle of faith.

That bird with its head in your lap makes you
Toss back your hair, showing us
Its torture. Maybe your risk is simply a way
Of spending faith. Neither the bird nor I believe you.

Yet, I believe the one sleeping
Beside you at night wears a face torn by branches,
& a pain up through the bones.

A face like the world: Distant, not part of you.

You blame the childhood of a man, the future
Stitched along a woman's lips. The frost in winter,
Peppering the leaves. You blame
The light delivered upon the snow, the smoke
Unraveling.

One year, you slept alone
Dividing your life into what touched you, & the world.
That is, what hurt you: Any woman,
Any man; A newspaper frozen in a tree; A late train.

Sometimes, blame breaks like faith to solitude.

You stood at the mirror. You took your hair in one hand,
& pulled it to the side, like a single, broken
Wing. You cut the left side, & the right. You clipped
The back like a boy's, a ragged curl along the neck.
Insight into the carnal drift of things.

Maybe you find a man who admires your rings.
Maybe you have lunch with an old pal, talk up
The past. The tidepools, the whales
Migrating up the coast. How you're both
Waiting for the storms dressing the sky to pass.

Waiting for the letter ending, *If these walks*
*By the lake will calm us, like these lovers we*
*Dismiss as children, & good soldiers.*

Maybe you learn from the anarchy of the trees,
Maybe you sit around waiting for the news:

At last this one, or that one, is free.

Everyone you know leaving such passionate debris.
Everyone going out at night to stand alone,
& in the rain. You run into a friend, at a party,
Or the loud weather of a bar, & you each pour out
Your nonsense. He says, *Sex is dialectic;*
*The will is blue, & malevolent, yet lithe in nature.*

So, you let go a whole cadenza of beliefs:

*The one-man bobsled was invented by Kropotkin;*
*The individual*
*Is sovereign; The will is the meat of the apple.*

You walk the gardens in the Park. The iris,
The glass chalets burning in the slow, red dusk.
The only prayer is to continue. To lean far
Out of the boat, & pick a dead bird off a wave.
This dialogue you refuse. Some city, where
You can finish out a life burning like another skin.
The bruises, open doors. You reach high
Into the lime tree, carving away a life. If risk is faith.
You blame the branches lacing my torn face,
The light in winter, stitched along the quays; the news,

The one beside you. The summer storms muting the bare trees.

# Notes

THIS: The poem takes as a source the Różewicz poem, In the Middle of Life.

FOUR O'CLOCK IN SUMMER: HOPE: For Fran. The Tanguy painting hangs in the Raymond Queneau collection in Paris. It is dated 1929.

SIX/NINE/FORTY-FOUR: Keith Douglas, British poet, active in the North African tank campaigns of WWII. Killed in the Normandy invasion.

DOLLS: The poem takes as a casual source Rilke's essay, Some Reflections on Dolls.

WEDDING PREPARATIONS IN THE COUNTRY: The title is taken from an unfinished story by Kafka.